THE SCIENCE OF
BASKETBALL

THE TOP 10 WAYS SCIENCE AFFECTS THE GAME

by Matt Chandler

Consultant:
Harold Pratt
President of Educational Consultants
Littleton, Colorado

CAPSTONE PRESS
a capstone imprint

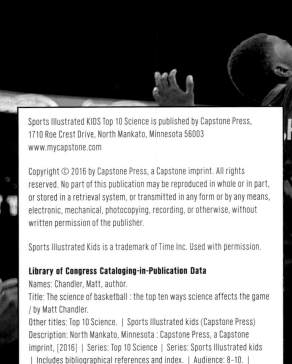

Sports Illustrated KIDS Top 10 Science is published by Capstone Press, 1710 Roe Crest Drive, North Mankato, Minnesota 56003 www.mycapstone.com

Library of Congress Cataloging-in-Publication Data
Names: Chandler, Matt, author.
Title: The science of basketball : the top ten ways science affects the game / by Matt Chandler.
Other titles: Top 10 Science. | Sports Illustrated kids (Capstone Press)
Description: North Mankato, Minnesota : Capstone Press, a Capstone imprint, [2016] | Series: Top 10 Science | Series: Sports Illustrated kids | Includes bibliographical references and index. | Audience: 8–10. | Audience: 4 to 6.
Identifiers: LCCN 2015035087
ISBN 9781491482209 (library binding)
ISBN 9781491486009 (pbk.)
ISBN 9781491486047 (ebook pdf)
Subjects: LCSH: Basketball–Juvenile literature. | Sports sciences–Juvenile literature.
Classification: LCC GV885.1 .C53 2016 | DDC 796.323–dc23
LC record available at http://lccn.loc.gov/2015035087

Editorial Credits
Adrian Vigliano, editor; Sarah Bennett, designer; Eric Gohl, media researcher; Lori Blackwell, production specialist

Photo Credits
Getty Images: AFP/George Frey, 24, Sports Illustrated/Greg Nelson, 11; Newscom: Cal Sport Media/Stephen Lew, 29, MCT/Chuck Myers, 13, USA Today Sports/Brace Hemmelgarn, 23, ZUMA Press/Kyndell Harkness, 17; Shutterstock: irin-k, 1; Sports Illustrated: Al Tielemans, 2, David E. Klutho, 4–5, 26, John W. McDonough, cover, 7, 8, 10, 15, 18, 20, Manny Millan, 21

Design Elements: Shutterstock

Printed in the United States of America, in North Mankato, Minnesota.
009221CGS1.

Table of Contents

▶ LeBron James

Michael Jordan, LeBron James, Larry Bird, Kobe Bryant—each player is a basketball superstar. They are known for their skills, but science helps set them apart. Science is an important factor behind Jordan's rings, Bird's legacy, James' MVP seasons, and Bryant's dominance. Every shot, block, dribble, and dunk is backed by the science of the game. What made Jordan jump so high? What was the key to Bird's outside shooting? How could Bryant dominate while still a teenager? What makes James almost unstoppable? Find out as we explore the game of basketball in ways you've never imagined!

Jump, Shoot, Score!

Shape of the Shot

When Golden State Warriors guard Stephen Curry pulls up and launches a three-point shot, it's a thing of beauty. For Curry to make his shot, he must judge how much **acceleration** he creates for the ball. He must also figure the amount of spin he creates with the shot. If Curry misjudges either factor he could overshoot or toss an air ball.

Players who understand these forces can use them to create extra spin on the ball. For Curry, that could mean adding some spin to bank in a floater off the glass for the game-winning basket!

acceleration ⟹ the change in the velocity of a body

▼ Stephen Curry only has seconds to take the perfect three-point shot.

Tim Duncan powers through an opposing defense to take his shot.

8

Gravitational Pull

Sir Isaac Newton's law of universal gravitation was published in 1687—more than 200 years before basketball was invented. But Newton might have made a good basketball player because he understood the importance of gravitational pull on every object.

Gravity plays a role in every basket or missed shot in the history of the game.

Gravity is constantly acting on all objects. San Antonio Spurs center Tim Duncan has made more than 10,000 baskets in his NBA career. Duncan has also missed nearly 10,000 shots.

When the ball leaves his hand, gravity begins pulling the ball toward the floor. This means the player must judge how high to shoot the ball to take gravity into account. The farther he is from the basket, the higher he must shoot the ball. This will allow the ball to still be above the rim by the time it reaches the basket. A player right under the basket can toss the ball so it barely clears the rim and let gravity pull it right through the hoop.

gravity ⟹ a force that pulls objects together

Angling for a Basket

New Orleans Pelicans forward Anthony Davis blocked two hundred shots during the 2014–15 season. At 6'10" (2 meters) Davis towers over many of his opponents. This forces players to shoot the ball with a high **arc** to get over his outstretched arms. But there is another reason a player may want to change the arc of his shot. The rim is 18 inches (46 centimeters) in diameter compared to the basketball, which is about 9.8 inches (24.1 centimeters) in diameter. The angle at which the ball arrives at the basket is very important. A high shot dropping down has a better chance of going in. A shot coming in with a lower arc effectively reduces the basket to an oval, decreasing the chances the shot is made.

◄ Los Angeles Lakers guard Jeremy Lin dodges a defender's block attempt as he drives to the rim.

arc ➡ a curved line, like a rainbow

The ball's path creates an arc.

▲ The perfect shot arc can help a shooter avoid multiple defenders.

Understanding angles is a big part of a player's success. Shoot at too low an angle and the shot can be blocked or clang off the rim. Float the ball too high, and it may react with too much bounce when it hits the rim. A ball dropped from 3 feet (.9 meters) up will bounce less than a ball that is dropped from 6 feet (1.8 meters) up. This means a ball shot at too high of an angle will have a higher bounce if it doesn't go in. That higher bounce could offer opponents more time to get an easy rebound.

Perfecting Ball Spin

It would be nice if every shot was "nothing but net," but many shots are banked off the glass or bounce off the rim and in. How a player like Chicago Sky forward Elena Delle Donne spins the ball as it leaves her hand determines how often these shots are successful.

There are two forces that slow down the ball once it is shot. Gravity is constantly pulling at the ball and bringing it down. Shooters learn how to work with gravity to precisely arc the ball toward the basket. Once the ball hits the rim or backboard, **friction** slows it even more.

When a shot with lots of backspin hits the rim, more of the energy is transferred from the ball to the basket. A ball that loses its energy naturally slows down. Players such as Delle Donne work to perfect the amount of backspin they put on the ball. The perfect spin gives a shooter more control in getting the ball to bounce into the basket.

▶ Elena Delle Donne works to keep her shooting form sharp in midair so she can create the perfect backspin.

friction ➠ a force produced when two objects rub against each other; friction slows down objects

Slam Science

Golden State Warriors guard Andre Iguodala has dunked the basketball more than 1,200 times in his NBA career. Iguodala appears to float as he palms the basketball and launches himself in the air toward the basket. While it may look like he is hanging in mid-air, he is actually being pulled down constantly by gravity, just like all objects. The floating effect is actually an **illusion** created by the science of the jump.

A player such as Iguodala prepares for a jump by running and picking up speed. The measurement of his speed and jumping direction is called **velocity**. Iguodala's velocity is greatest at the moment he jumps. As he leaves the ground, gravity continues pulling him back to the floor. As Iguodala reaches the peak of his jump, his upward velocity slows down. Eventually his speed downward picks up again as he drops back to the floor. Studies show that a player spends 71 percent of his airtime in the top half of a jump, and only 29 percent in the bottom half. Because more time is spent in the top half of the jump, it creates an illusion that the player is floating.

illusion ➤ something that appears to be real but isn't

velocity ➤ a measurement of both the speed and direction an object is moving

▲ Andre Iguodala makes a huge, gliding dunk look effortless.

The Dribble

Being able to dribble effectively gives a player the ability to control both the ball and the pace of the entire game. Minnesota Lynx forward Maya Moore does this when she brings the ball up the court. In the backcourt she dribbles the ball high, with her hands up at her waist or higher. But as she gets into traffic, she adjusts. Now her dribble is much lower to the ground. She adjusts because she wants to use physics to her advantage.

Coming up the court, Moore uses very little force to push the ball down, and the dribble has a low velocity. She knows that when it is time to drive for the basket she must dribble harder. By dribbling lower to the court, Moore shortens the distance the ball travels when it leaves her hand. When the ball hits the ground, the ball bounces back with a force equal to that which Moore used when dribbling it down. By using more force and shortening the distance the ball is traveling as it bounces, Moore gives defenders much less time to attempt a steal.

▶ Maya Moore keeps her dribble high as she moves up the court.

AIR EQUALITY

Every basketball in the NBA and WNBA is required to be inflated with between 7.5 and 8.5 pounds of air pressure per square inch. A properly inflated ball is firm to the touch. But what happens if a ball has less air in it? If two balls are dribbled with the same velocity, the ball with more air will bounce higher.

When air is pumped into a basketball, it pushes against the inside of the ball. The basketball has a limited amount of space for the air, so when the ball gets full the air pressure rises, making the ball hard. When a player dribbles, the air is pushed even tighter together when it hits the floor.

Isaac Newton's Third Law of Motion states that for every action there is an equal and opposite reaction. When a properly inflated basketball hits the hardwood, the ball flattens slightly before it bounces back. Imagine it like a spring on your bed. When you dive onto the bed, you push the springs down and they recoil, tossing you up into the air. The harder you dive, the farther you will be launched back into the air. In the same way, the harder a basketball is dribbled, the more it will flatten and spring back in the air.

Chris Paul uses the speed of his jump to create the perfect layup.

The Perfect Layup

When Los Angeles Clippers guard Chris Paul drives to the hoop for a layup, he makes it look easy. Some of the tools that make Paul successful can be explained by discoveries made centuries ago by Italian astronomer Galileo Galilei.

When a player shoots a layup, he often goes airborne well before reaching the basket. Since the basket is in front of the player, it seems that he will have to push the ball forward when he shoots. But a player who does that will usually see his shot bang off the glass.

Galileo did an experiment and discovered than an object that is dropped from a person in motion doesn't fall straight down. Instead, the object continues to move in the same direction and speed as the person who dropped it. A skilled basketball player knows how to use this when coming in for a layup. When an airborne player lets go of the ball, it continues to travel toward the basket at the same speed without any forward push. Instead of pushing his shot forward, he must aim his jump, release the ball toward the basket, and let physics take it from there.

Does Momentum Matter?

Any object in motion has **momentum**. The amount of momentum an object has is determined by multiplying the **mass** of the object and its velocity.

A basketball game is full of momentum. A basketball has momentum after it is shot. A player also has momentum as he or she drives through the lane. Because the player's mass is greater than the ball's, the player will usually have greater momentum. Oklahoma City Thunder guard Russell Westbrook weighs 200 pounds (90.7 kilograms). The average NBA ball weighs 22 ounces (.62 kilograms). With such a great difference in mass, it's easy to see why Westbrook has more momentum on the court.

▲ Russell Westbrook

momentum ⇒ a property of a moving object determined by multiplying its mass and velocity

mass ⇒ the amount of material in an object

The science of momentum plays a huge role in a basketball game. A player can use his size and speed to gain momentum while driving through the lane. Defenders may think twice about stepping in front of a driving player with lots of momentum. Defensive hesitation can give the shooter an advantage and may open up lanes to the basket.

Momentum can also work against a player. The more momentum something has, the more difficult it is to get it to change directions. A player chasing a loose ball may lose control and find that his or her momentum carries him past the sidelines and even into a fan's lap.

DRESS FOR SUCCESS

Shoe companies want you to think you will be a better player if you wear their brand. But did wearing Air Jordan shoes actually make Michael Jordan jump higher?

NBA players such as Jordan jump high because of the energy stored in the muscles of their legs. When they push off and leap, that energy propels them into the air. Players with strong calf muscles jump with their weight on their toes. Because jumping is based on the body's use of stored energy, the padding in a shoe can actually hurt a player's jump. The soft padding is meant to cushion a player's foot. But it also absorbs some of the energy from the muscles, making the leap less powerful.

21

Free Throw Form

Some coaches tell players not to overthink their free throws. But the brain plays a big part in free-throw success.

Shooting free throws is about repetition. Did you ever notice that many players have rituals when they shoot foul shots? They dribble the same number of times. They might spin the ball twice in their hands or do a few deep knee bends before they shoot. All of this repetition helps a player's brain.

The part of the brain that controls conscious thought is called the cerebral cortex. But when a player like Los Angeles Lakers guard Kobe Bryant steps to the foul line, another part of his brain known as the cerebellum helps him make the shots. As Bryant practiced and mastered free throw shooting, his brain adjusted and his cerebellum began to help control his technique and shot. The cerebellum works lightning fast and is effective on tasks that involve repetition.

▸ Kobe Bryant's body and brain work together on every free throw.

Every free throw is taken from the same spot, at the same distance, with no defense. This means what it takes to make the shot is identical every time. Storing this information in the brain and then repeating the perfect motion is what makes a great free throw shooter.

distance from rim = 15 feet (4.6 meters)

height of rim = 10 feet (3 meters)

The Science of Defense

Thief on the Court

Defense plays a huge part in a team's success. Former Utah Jazz point guard John Stockton was an incredible defensive thief. He collected 3,265 steals in his NBA career. Stealing the ball is all about anticipating what your opponent is going to do next and using your instincts to go for the ball at the exact right moment.

One study found that the human brain reacts correctly on instinct as much as 90 percent of the time. Stockton's brain stored up mountains of information on every opponent. This information created the foundation for his instincts. Without thinking, his brain took in what his opponent was doing and compared this information to what it already knew. In a split second, Stockton could react and go for the steal. If he had taken time to consciously think things through, the player would likely get past him. But using his instincts led him to thousands of steals.

◀ John Stockton holds the NBA record for most career steals.

Rejected

At 7 feet (2.13 meters) tall, Portland Trail Blazers center Robin Lopez is built to block shots. But it wasn't height alone that allowed him to block more than 1.4 shots per game during the 2014–15 season. Timing is key to blocking a shot. Lopez must anticipate when his opponent is going to shoot. He then has to time his jump just right.

Basketball players rely on the muscle memory of the cerebellum to help them shoot. This communication between the brain and the central nervous system tells a player how hard to shoot the ball because he has done it thousands of times before. Muscle memory can help defenders like Lopez as well. Lopez's brain and nervous system know how much energy to use when making the jump. Lopez's body also knows when to jump based on stored information in his brain. The combination of instincts, muscle memory, and height make him a nightmare for shooters.

◄ With the right timing, Robin Lopez can quickly deny an opponent's shot attempt.

Crowd Participation

There are 10 seconds left in the game and Houston Rockets center Dwight Howard has the ball with his team down by one point. The home fans are on their feet screaming so loud that the building feels like it's shaking. Players talk about home-court advantage, but can a cheering crowd actually help Howard make his shot?

One study found a direct link between home crowd noise and the success of a team. No one is exactly sure how a crowd helps a team, but some scientists think crowd noise produces a physical reaction. These scientists tested players in home and away games and found that the players' bodies produced more testosterone at home than on the road. The scientists concluded that the extra testosterone makes players push harder, possibly leading to more victories.

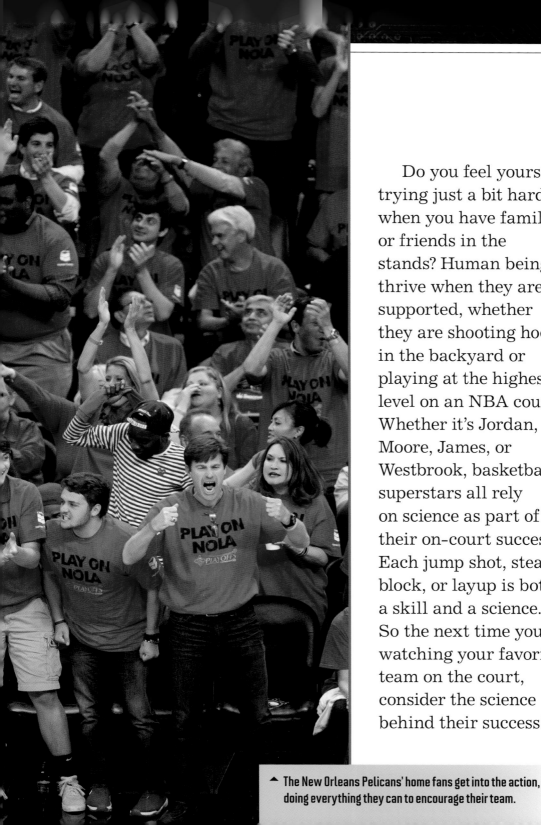

Do you feel yourself trying just a bit harder when you have family or friends in the stands? Human beings thrive when they are supported, whether they are shooting hoops in the backyard or playing at the highest level on an NBA court. Whether it's Jordan, Moore, James, or Westbrook, basketball superstars all rely on science as part of their on-court success. Each jump shot, steal, block, or layup is both a skill and a science. So the next time you're watching your favorite team on the court, consider the science behind their success!

▲ The New Orleans Pelicans' home fans get into the action, doing everything they can to encourage their team.

GLOSSARY

acceleration (ak-sel-uh-RAY-shuhn) ➞ the change in the velocity of a body

arc (ARK) ➞ a curved line, like a rainbow

friction (FRIK-shuhn) ➞ a force produced when two objects rub against each other; friction slows down objects.

gravity (GRAV-uh-tee) ➞ a force that pulls objects together

illusion (i-LOO-zhuhn) ➞ something that appears to be real but isn't

mass (MASS) ➞ the amount of material in an object

momentum (moh-MEN-tuhm) ➞ a property of a moving object determined by multiplying its mass and velocity

velocity (vuh-LOSS-uh-tee) ➞ a measurement of both the speed and direction an object is moving

READ MORE

Bethea, Nikole Brooks. *The Science of Basketball with Max Axiom, Super Scientist*. North Mankato, Minn.: Capstone Press, 2016.

Graubart, Norman. *The Science of Basketball*. New York: PowerKids Press, 2016.

Slade, Suzanne. *Basketball, How It Works*. Mankato Minn.: Capstone Press, 2010.

INTERNET SITES

FactHound offers a safe, fun way to find Internet sites related to this book. All of the sites on FactHound have been researched by our staff.

Here's all you do:

Visit *www.facthound.com*

Type in this code: 9781491482209

 **Super-cool stuff!** Check out projects, games and lots more at **www.capstonekids.com**

INDEX